This book belongs to

olivia

Silly Billy!

How do you confuse
a Silly Billy?
Offer him two spades
and ask him to take
his pick.

Why did the Silly Billy
fall out of his window?
He was ironing his curtains.

Did you hear about the
fool who kept on going
round saying no?
Silly Billy: No.

Did you hear about
the Silly Billy who took
up tap dancing?
He fell into the sink.

Did you hear about
the Silly Billy who
swallowed a light bulb?
After he spat it out
he said he felt delighted.

Did you hear about
the Silly Billy who would
plow his field with a
steamroller?
He said he wanted to
grow mashed potatoes.

What did Silly Billy
do when he saw a
sign on a bench saying
wet paint?
He got a bucket of
water and poured it
over the bench.

How does Silly Billy
call his dog?
He puts two fingers in
his mouth and shouts
"Barny!"

Five Silly Billy's have got lost on this page, find them and then colour the page in!

If you've made it look very wonderful, take a picture and show your friends.

Jokes to tell Teacher

What's a pirates favourite lesson?
Arrrr!

What do elves learn at school?
The elf-abet.

Did you hear about the boy who took the school bus home?
The teachers made home bring it back.

Why did they nose hate school?
He kept getting picked on.

How did you find school today?
I just got off the bus and it was there.

Why was the broom late for school?
It overswept.

Who invented fractions?
Henry the Eighth.

Why did the teacher turn the light on?
Because her class was so dim.

How do bees get to school?
On the school buzz.

Teacher: You aren't paying attention. Are you having trouble hearing?
Pupil: No miss, I'm having trouble listening.

Jokes to tell Teacher

Did you hear about the farmer who won the Nobel prize? He was out standing in his field.

Did you hear about the man who couldn't tell the difference between toothpaste and putty? His windows fell out.

What happened to the two bed bugs who fell in love? They got married in the spring.

How did the car get a puncture? From the fork in the road.

Why did the nose cross the road? Because he was getting picked on.

Surgeon: Just relax, there's no need to worry? Patient: But it's my first operation and I'm really nervous. Surgeon: Well, it's my first operation and I'm not worried at all.

Where does Robbin Hood by his flowers? At Sherwood Florists.

Why did the poet have to get a proper job? Because he realised rhyme doesn't pay.

How easy is it to please a greedy person? It's a piece of cake.

Teacher: What does coincidence mean? Pupil: That's funny, I was just going to ask you that?

Silly Family's

Dad: Why are you home from school so early?
Son: I was the only one who could answer the question.
Dad: Well, done son what was the question?
Son: Who broke the window.

Son: Dad why is your face so wrinkly?
Dad: They're not wrinkles, they're laughter lines.
Son: Trust me, nothing's that funny.

Dad: Why does everyone call you teachers pet?
Son: She keeps me in a cage.

Sister: I look awful in this dress, can someone give me a compliment?
Brother: You have perfect eyesight!

Brother: Whats the difference between a hippos bottom and a postbox?
Sister: I don't know.
Brother: Well, I'd better not give you my letters to post, then.

Brother: What do you mean by telling all your friends I'm an idiot?
Sister: I'm sorry, I didn't know it was a secret.

Son: Mum, can I have another glass of water, please?
Mum: Thats the fifth one since you went to bed, why are you so thirsty?
Son: I'm not thirsty, my bedrooms on fire!

Son: Mum, what's the most dangerous thing about driving?
Mum: The nut behind the steering wheel.

Silly Family's

Why do parents carry their babies?
Because their babies aren't big enough to carry their parents.

Dad: You promised me You'd make 100 per cent effort this week.
Son: I did! Monday 25 per cent Tuesday 35, 15 on Wednesday and Thursday and 10 on Friday!

Why was the toast unhappy after marrying the margarine?
She was expecting someone butter.

Dad: When your grandpa was in the army he saved the whole regiment.
Son: What did he do?
Dad: He shot the cook.

Son: Dad do you have a good memory?
Dad: Yes son why do you ask?
Son: Oh, I broke your shaving mirror.

Dad: Son why didn't you mow the lawn last week?
Son: I broke my leg last week.
Dad: That's a lame excuse.

Sing to Mum!
For she's a jolly good fellow
Her hearts is sweeter Than gello
Her skins as soft as marshmallow
And so say all of us!
And so say all of us!

Daft Jokes!

What do campers need
after a big drink?
A Tea-pee.

What do you call
a baby ant?
An infant.

Who carry's a
big sack and
goes oh, oh, oh?
Sant Claus walking
backwards.

How do you
start a soft
toy race?
Ready, Teddy Go!

Where does a
boat go when
it's sick?
To the dock.

What's the best
time to go to
a dentist?
Tooth-hurty.

What did the duck
say when he fell over
in a China shop.
I hope I didn't
quack any.

What's big and yellow
And arrives early every
morning to brighten
your moms day?
The school bus.

Silly Cat & Mouse

What cat should you never play cards with.
A cheetah.

How do cats keep their soda cold?
With mice-cubes.

What do you get if you cross a cat with a lemon?
A sourpuss.

What do cats do when they buy a new home?
They celebrate with mouse warming party

What do cats eat for breakfast?
Mice-krispies.

What's grey has four legs and a trunk?
A mouse going on holiday.

What's brown has four legs and a trunk?
A mouse coming back from holiday.

What cat grows in a garden?
A dandelion.

What did the mouse say when he broke his teeth?
Hard cheese.

Once you found eight
lost kittens, then you can
colour in the picture.

Knock, Knock!

Knock, Knock!
Who's there?
Cornflakes.
Cornflakes who?
I'll tell you next week
it's a cereal.

Knock, Knock!
Who's there?
Pudding.
Pudding who?
Pudding your pants
after your trousers is
not a good idea.

Knock, Knock!
Who's there?
Reed.
Reed who?
Reed all about it
a boy opens his door.

Knock, Knock!
Who's there?
Little old lady.
Little old lady Who?
I didn't know you
could yodel.

Knock, Knock!
Who's there?
Duck.
Duck who?
JUST DUCK! There's a
missile coming!

Knock, Knock!
Who's there?
Tamara.
Tamara who?
Tamara I'll use
your window.

Knock, Knock! Who's there?
Mary Lee. Mary Lee who?
Mary-Lee, Mary Lee, life is But a dream.
Row, row , row your boat...

Knock, Knock!

Knock, Knock!
Who's there?
Dawn.
Dawn who?
Dawn just stand there
open the door!

Knock, Knock!
Who's there?
Nadia.
Nadia who?
Nadia business.

Knock, Knock!
Who's there?
Arge and Tina.
Arge and Tina who?
Arge and Tina
just won the cup!

Knock, Knock!
Who's there?
Kay.
Kay who?
Kay sera sera!

Knock, Knock!
Who's there?
Justin.
Justin who.
Justin time, it's
starting to rain.

Knock, Knock!
Who's there?
Abby.
Abby who?
Abby birthday
to you!

Who's there? Joo. Joo who?
Joo-who let the dogs out?

Best Jokes!

Where was grandad when the
lights went out?
In the dark.

Did you hear about the girl
who slept with her head under
her pillow?
The fairies took all her teeth away.

What cowboy lives at the bottom
of the sea?
Billy the Squid.

How did the tap dancer break
his leg?
He fell into the sink.

Where did Napoleon keep his
armies?
Up his sleevies.

Best Jokes!

What happened when the lion
who ate the man?
He felt funny.

Where would you weigh a whale?
At a whale-weigh station.

What's wrong with a man with
jelly in one ear and sponge in another?
He's a trifle death.

What did Tarzan say when he saw
elephants coming over the hill?
Here come the elephants.

What did the first mind reader
say to the second mind reader?
You're all right how am I?

Best Jokes!

Mum: Why are you crying?
Boy: Dad hit his thumb with the hammer.
Mum: Knowing you I'm surprised you
didn't laugh.
Boy: That's the trouble I did.

What did the earwig say
when he fell off the wall?
Earwig go again.

How does a witch tell the time?
With a witch watch.

Who did Dracula marry?
The girl necks door.

I can make you talk like a
Red indian?
How?
See, I told you.

Cross The Road Jokes

Why did the rooster
cross the road?
To cock-a-doodle-doo something.

Why did the dog
cross the road?
To get out of the barking lot.

Why did the cat
cross the road?
Because it's owner told it
not to do it.

Why did the chicken
cross the road, roll in dirt
and then walk back?
Because it was a dirty double crosser.

Cross The Road Jokes

Why did the germ
cross the lab?
To get to the other slide

Why did the fish
cross the ocean?
To get to the other tide.

Why did the hedgehog
cross the road?
To see his flat mate.

Why did the cow
cross the road?
to get to the udder side.

Silly Pirates

How much do
pirate earrings cost?
A buccaneer.

Why does it take
a pirate so long
to learn the alphabet?
Because he spends too
long at C.

Why did Captain Hook
cross the road?
To get to the second
hand shop.

What lies at the
bottom of the ocean
and twitches?
A nervous wreck.

What's orange and
sounds like parrot?
Carrot.

Why are Pirates
called pirates?
Because they aaaarrrrr!

Why couldn't the
pirate play cards?
Because he was standing
on the deck.

What did the pirate
name his daughter?
Peggy.

What did the
dyslexic pirate say?
RRRRRRA1

Where can you find
a pirate that's lost
his wooden leg?
Right where you left
him.

What's the difference
between a hungry pirate
and a drunken pirate?
One got a rumbling tummy,
and the others got a
tumbling rummy.

Silly pirate drank to much rum and lost 11 diamonds from his treasure chest. You've ten minutes to find them all, or walk the plank.

Best Jokes!

Did you hear about the cat
that married a glove?
They had mittens.

What's the difference between a wet
day and a lion with tooth-ache?
One's pouring with rain; the other's
roaring with pain.

What goes dot-dot-dot-croak?
Morse toad.

What do you call a hot
sausage in space?
An unidentified fry Object. (UFO).

Two aerials meet on a roof, fall in
love and get married. The ceremony was
rubbish but the reception was fantastic.

What's the hardest part of milking
a gerbil?
Getting the bucket under it.

Best Jokes!

Boy: I think my teacher loves me.
Mum: How can you tell?
Boy: She keeps putting kisses by my sums.

What do you get if you
cross an owl with a skunk?
A bird that smells but doesn't
give a hoot.

The Wally family were driving to
see Stonehenge. They saw a sign saying
'Stonehenge Left'. They were very angry
and drove straight home.

I used to be indecisive-
now I'm not so sure.

'Can you help me?' a worried
man asked the animal shelter officer.
'I'm looking for a stray dog with one
eye.' 'Would it help if you used both
eyes?' yawned the officer.

Silly Books

You'll find these books in a Silly Library.

Coffee maker
by Phil Turr

REMEMBERING ANNIVERSARIES
BY BETTY WONT

Bull Fighting
by Mat Adore

Great Breakfast
By Hammond Deggs

Leaky Boat
By I . C. King

Building Wigwams
By T. P

Long Winter
By Ron. E. Nose

Lovely Breakfast
by Roland Jam

How to keep pigs
By Chris p. Bacon

LIFE IN PRISON
BY ROBBIN BANKS

Blushing
By Rosie Cheeks

OLD SCHOOL RECORDING
BY CASS ETE

Antibiotics
By Penny Silling

Nosey neighbours
by Annette Curtain

Silly Jobs

Why was the postman fed up? He got the sack on his first day.

What did they call Postman Pat when he retired? Pat.

How do you become a professor? By degrees.

How do greengrocer's mend the holes in their trousers? With cabbage patches.

Why are train drivers always anxious? Because their jobs always on the line.

Where do generals keep their armies? Up their sleevies.

What kind of fish do fishermen catch at night? Starfish.

Why do surgeons wear masks? So that if they make a mistake, nobody will know who did it.

What's the most exhausting month to be a soldier? The month of March.

What happens when the Queen burps? She issues a royal pardon.

What kind of training do you need to be a waste collector? None- you just pick it up as you go along.

Silly Riddles

What's hidden in the pictures?

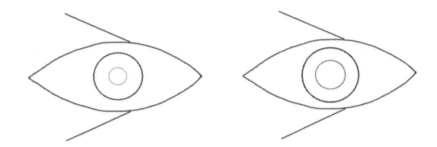

Two Mexicans rowing two boats.

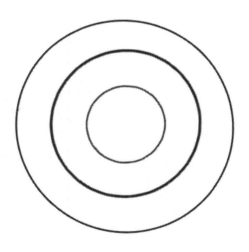

A large Mexican wearing a sombrero.

Silly Riddles

What's hidden in the pictures?

After the python met the zookeeper.

Two men and a vase.

Best Jokes!

Did you hear about the magic tractor?
It went down the lane and turned into a field.

How does an Eskimo build his house?
Igloos it together.

How many ears did Captain Kirk have?
Three: a left ear, a right
ear and a final frontier.

What do you call a camel with
no humps?
Humphrey.
What do you a camel with three humps.
Lumpy.

What did the Martian say to the
petrol pump?
Take your finger out of your ear
when I'm talking to you.

How do you know flowers are lazy?
You always find them in bed.

Best Jokes!

Boy: I think my teacher loves me.
Mum: How can you tell?
Boy: She keeps putting kisses by my sums.

What do you get if you
cross an owl with a skunk?
A bird that smells but doesn't
give a hoot.

The Wally family were driving to
see Stonehenge. They saw a sign saying
'Stonehenge Left'. They were very angry
and drove straight home.

I used to be indecisive-
now I'm not so sure.

'Can you help me?' a worried
man asked the animal shelter officer.
'I'm looking for a stray dog with one
eye.' 'Would it help if you used both
eyes?' yawned the officer.

Best Jokes!

Brother: 'Why are you cutting
up that block of ice?'
Sister: 'So that it will fit into the
ice cube tray of course.'

Boy: 'Dad what do you do for a job?'
Dad: 'It's very important, I have thousands
of men under me.'
Mum: 'Your Dad works in a cemetery.'

Teacher: 'How was your holiday
in Switzerland Tom?''Was the
scenery lovely?'
Tom: 'It was hard to see the scenery,
the mountains kept getting in the way.'

Brother: 'Birthday cake gives me heartburn.'
Sister: 'Try taking the candles off
before eating it next time.'

Silly Sea

Why was the mermaid
so bitter?
She grew up with
a ship on her shoulder.

Why do oceans
never go out of
style?
Because they're
always current.

Why did Noah
only catch two fish?
He only had
two worms.

Doctor, Doctor,
I smell like a fish.
Oh you poor sole.

Why was the lobster
sent to prison?
He kept on pinching
things.

Why do fish swim
in salt water?
Because pepper makes
them sneeze.

What fish makes
a goes with ice cream?
A jellyfish.

What day do fish
hate most?
Fryday.

What's a sharks
favourite game?
Swallow the leader.

What do you call a fishes date?
His gill-friend.

What do you call a boats date?
Her buoy-friend.

Silly Sea

When is fishing
not a good way
to relax?
When your a worm.

What kind of fish
can't swim?
Dead ones.

How do you
communicate with
a fish?
Drop him a line.

What runs but
never walks?
Water.

How do you chop
waves?
You don't you cut
them in half, with
a sea saw.

What did the ocean
say to the shore?
Nothing it just waved.

What do you get
if you cross a fish
with an elephant?
Swimming trunks.

What cats love water?
Octopusses.

Why did the oyster
go to university.
Because he had pearls
of wisdom.

Why did the crab
blush?
Because the sea-weed.

Sam: If frozen water
is iced water, what is
frozen ink?
Jim: Iced ink.
Sam: I know you do!

What did the useless fisherman catch?
A cold.
See if you can spot his rod.

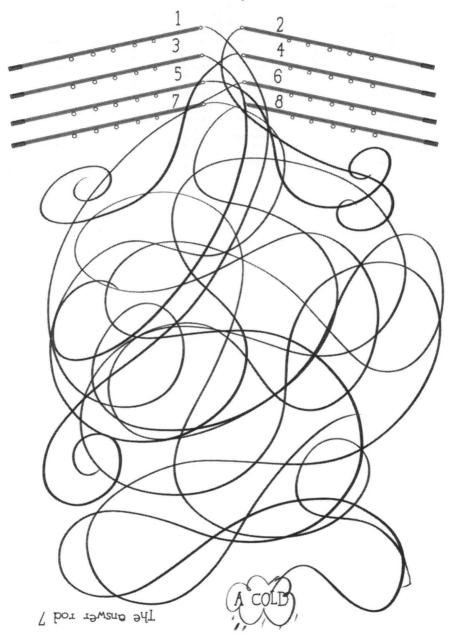

The answer rod 7

Find ten seahorse
shadows then colour
In the coral sea!

Knock, Knock!

Knock, Knock!
Who's there?
Pig.
Pig who?
Pig me up at four
and don't be late!

Knock, Knock!
Who's there?
Goat.
Goat who?
Goat to the door,
open it and
you'll see.

Knock, Knock!
Who's there?
Abee.
Abee who?
Abeecd E F G.

Knock, Knock!
Who's there?
Gorilla.
Gorilla who?
Gorilla me a burger,
I'm starving!

Knock, Knock!
Who's there?
Lion.
Lion who?
Lion on the sofa
all day is lazy, open
the door.

Knock, Knock!
Who's there?
Cook.
Cook who?
Cuckoo have you
been eating
bird seed?

Knock, Knock! Who's there? Berry.
Berry who? Berry glad to see you,
NOW LET ME IN!

Knock, Knock!

Knock, Knock!
Who's there?
Mice.
Mice who?
Mice to meet you,
cat you later!

Knock, Knock!
Who's there?
Radio.
Radio who?
Rad-io not,
here I come!

Knock, Knock!
Who's there?
Peas Who?
Peas to meet you,
lettuce in.

Knock, Knock!
Who's there?
Man ooher
Man ooher who?
Man-ooher on your
door step clean it up!

Knock, Knock!
Who's there?
Hawaii.
Hawaii who?
I'm fine, Hawaii you?

Knock, Knock!
Who's there?
Egg.
Egg who?
Egg-cited to
meet you.

Knock, Knock! Who's there? You.
You who? You-who, I'm still waiting.

Waiter, Waiter!

Waiter, What's this fly doing on my ice cream?
Waiter: Looks like it's skiing, Sir.

Waiter, This food is awful! Please get me the manager!
Waiter: He won't eat it either, sir.

Waiter, there appears to be a dead wasp in m soup.
Waiter: Yes, Sir, they're not very good swimmers.

Waiter, This steak taste funny.
Waiter: Then why aren't you laughing?

Waiter: This coffee taste like mud.
That doesn't surprise me, it was only ground a few moments ago.

Waiter, My wife wants to know if you serve frogs legs?
Waiter: Yes, Sir, tell her to take a seat, we serve anyone here sir.

Waiter, Have you got chicken legs?
Waiter: No, Sir, it's just the way I walk.

Waiter, is there soup on the menu?
Yes, let me wipe it off.

Waiter, you've got your thumb in my soup!
Waiter: Don't worry, Sir it's not very hot.

Waiter, Waiter!

Waiter, what do you call this?
Waiter: It's bean soup, sir.
Man: I don't care what it's been- what is it now?

Waiter: How did you find your steak?
Man: Well I just moved a chip and it was there.

Waiter, will my pizza be long?
Waiter: No, sir, it will be round.

Waiter, this egg is bad!
Waiter: Don't blame me, sir,
I only laid the table.

Waiter, There's a fly on my spaghetti.
Don't worry, sir, that spider on your bread will get him.

Waiter, my plates all wet!
Waiter: That's your soup, sir.

Waiter, I've just found a slug on my salad.
Waiter: Don't worry, sir, won't charge you any extra.

Waiter, why on earth is there a footprint on my steak?
Waiter: You did ask me to step on it, sir.

Waiter: What will you have, sir?
Man: Steak and kiddy pie, please.
Waiter: You mean steak and kidney pie, sir.
Man: I said kiddly, diddle I?

Cross The Road Jokes

Why did the duck
cross the road?
To prove he wasn't chicken.

Why did the turtle
cross the road?
To get to the shell station.

What happened when the elephant
crossed the road?
He stepped on a chicken.

Why did the chewing gum
cross the road?
Because it was stuck on the
chickens foot.

Cross The Road Jokes

Why did the fox
cross the road?
He was following the chicken.

Why did the chicken
cross the road?
Because it was a free range chicken

Why did the rubber chicken
cross the road?
To stretch its legs.

Why wouldn't the bike
cross the road?
Because it was two-tired.

Guess The Creature?

Strange named creatures!

Blue-footed booby

A bird from Peru.

Laughing jackass

Bird New Zealand.

Pudu

Small deer.

Bongo

Antelope.

Obese Lilly weevil

Beetle.

Purple Grackle

Bird USA.

Golden-rumped tinkerbird

Bird Congo.

Aye-aye

Lemur.

Tiny tuco-tuco

Rodent.

Gang gang cockatoo

Bird Australia.

Aha ha

Wasp.

Spotted thick knee

Bird Ethiopia.

Find six owl heads, then make
this page look beautiful.

Silly Animal Facts

Squirrels plant thousands of new trees each year by forgetting where they put their acorns.

Cows can have best friends. Maybe they go to the moovies together!

The Gentoo penguin proposes to his life mate with a pebble. It's less expensive than a gold ring!

Macaques monkeys in Japan, use coins to buy vending machine snacks.

Puffins mate for life. They make their homes on cliff sides and always set aside room for their toilet.

Seahorses mate for life, and when they travel they hold each others' tails.

Dogs' nose prints are as unique as human fingerprints and can be used to identify them.

Crows are so intelligent they can play pranks on each other.

Butterflies taste with their feet. Yuck!

Silly Animals

Is your dog fond of children?
Well, yes but he prefers tinned dog food.

Why wouldn't the lady buy a duck egg?
In case it had a quack in it.

Why can't you hide a leopard?
Because he's always spotted.

How does an elephant get down from a tree?
He sits on a leaf and waits till autumn.

Hickory dickory dock,
Two mouse ran up a clock.
The clock struck one but the other escaped with minor injuries.

What do you call a chicken in a shellsuit?
An egg.

What should you do if you meet a blue whale?
Try and cheer it up.

Why do cows lie down when it's cold?
To keep each udder warm.

What's black and white and red all over?
A penguin falling down the stairs.

Silly Animals

What do you call a cow that lives in an igloo?
An Eskimoo.

Where can you find a cat with no legs?
Wherever you left it.

What's the best way to catch a squirrel?
Climb up a tree and act like a nut.

What do you call a three legged donkey?
A wonkey.

What do you call a man with a rabbit up his jumper?
Warren.

Why did the farmer call his pig ink?
Because he kept on running out of the pen.

What goes dot-dot-dash-dash-squeak.

What do you get if you cross a frog with a ferry?
A hopper craft.

Did you her about the frog who's car broke down?
He got Toad away.

What time do ducks wake up?
At the quack of dawn.

What do you call a camel without a hump?
Humphrey.

Silly Animals

Why is a puppy good at DIY? Because he's always doing little jobs around the house.

Why did the pony cough? Because he was a little horse.

What do you call a pig that does karate? A pork chop.

Did you hear about the two birds that fell in love? They became tweethearts.

What's black and white and makes a lot of noise? A penguin with a drum kit.

What do you get if you cross an skunk with an owl? Someone who stinks but doesn't give a hoot.

What bird is always out of breath? A puffin.

What's black and white eats like a horse? A zebra.

How do horses propose? On bended neigh.

Find the 22 hidden fox's in ten minutes!

Silly Riddles

What's hidden in the pictures?

The face of a man and the word liar.

An Elephant leg illusion.

Silly Riddles

What's hidden in the pictures?

A man playing saxophone and a woman.

An Indian and a Eskimo cave.

Doctor, doctor!

Doctor, Doctor,
My eyesight is getting worse.
It certainly is this is a chip shop.

Doctor, Doctor,
I've swallowed a watch.
Don't worry, as time passes you'll feel better.

Doctor, Doctor,
I keep thinking I'm a sewing machine.
Oh, that's funny, you've got me in stitches.

Doctor, Doctor,
Please help me, I can't stop shaking.
Do you drink a lot?
Not really I spill most of it.

A man walks into a doctors office. He has a carrot stuck up his nose, a banana sticking out of one ear, and a cucumber sticking out of the other.
The doctor takes one look at him an says, "you're not eating properly."

Doctor, Doctor,
I feel like a very slow boomerang.
I'll try catch and you tomorrow.

Doctor, Doctor,
I'm frightened of squirrels.
You must be nuts!

Doctor, Doctor,
Can you help me out?
Certainly, what way did you come in?

Why did the clown go to the doctors?
Because he was feeling a little funny.

Doctor, doctor!

Doctor, Doctor,
I'm afraid of the light.
You must be a bit dim.

Doctor, Doctor,
If you can't see me
now I'm leaving.
Calm down, what's wrong
with you?
I have a serious wait
problem.

Doctor, Doctor,
Everyone thinks I'm
invisible.
Who said that?

Jim: I keep seeing
fuzzy spots in front
of my eyes.
Sam: Have you seen
a doctor?
Jim: No just fuzzy spots.

Doctor, Doctor,
I keep thinking I look
like an Octopus.
How long has this been
on for?
Since I was a little squid.

Doctor, Doctor,
I'm losing my memory.
How long has this been
going on for?
How long has what
been going on from?

Doctor, Doctor,
I think I'm Donald
duck.
How long have these
Disney spells been
going on for?

Doctor, Doctor,
I swallowed your
surgeries clock.
Stop wasting my time!

When do doctors get angry?
When they've run out of patients!

Silly Space!

What did the alien say to the tree?
Take me to your cedar!

How does the man on the moon cut his toenails?
Eclipse them.

Knock, knock.
Who's there?
Cosmos.
Cosmos who?
Cosmos of us are outside, you should let us in!

How do spacemen hold up their pants?
With asteroid belts.

Hey did the earthling fall in love with the alien?
Because she was out of this world.

How did the earthling feel when an alien landed with eight lasers for arms?
Stunned.

How do you turn a regular scientist into a mad scientist?
Stand on her toes!

Knock, knock.
Who's there?
Apollo.
Apollo who?
Apollo-gize for not answering sooner.

Silly Space!

Why did the atom cross the road?
Because it was time to split.

Why couldn't the astronauts book a room on the moon?
Because it was full.

Why wouldn't the astronauts book a table at the restaurant?
Because it had no atmosphere!

Why did Captain Kirk sneak into the ladies room?
Because ho wanted to go where no man had gone before.

How does Darth Vader know what you're getting for Christmas?
He feels your presents.

What did the sun say when it was introduced to the earth?
Pleased to heat you.

What did the alien say to the cat?
Take me to your littler.

What robot always takes the longest route?
R2 Detour.

Colour this Space page
in using only four colours,
and make it look amazing!

Cops n Robbers

What did the policeman say to his belly?
You're under a vest.

Did you hear about the sheep dog trials?
Two of the dogs we're found guilty.

A man rushed into a bank, then pointed his finger at the cashier, saying "This is a muck-up!" 'Don't you mean stick-up?' Said the cashier. 'No' said the man, 'muck-up I forgot my gun.

Knock, knock.
Who's there?
Irish stew.
Irish stew who?
Irish stew in the name of the law.

Where do policemen live?
Letsby Avenue.

What happened to man who stole a calendar?
He got twelve months.

The local wig shop was burgled last night, 200 wigs were stolen.
Police are now combing the area.

Policeman: Listen buddy this is a one way st.
Motorist: That's alright I'm only going one way.

Judge: What were you doing in the bank at 3 a.m. when the police entered?
Defendant: I was making a bolt for the door.

Silly Signs

CAUTION
THIS SIGN
HAS SHARP
EDGES

Warning
Please look under
your vehicles
for penguins

BEWARE

WILD ANIMALS/
CHILDREN

Wash & Vacum
Senior Citizens
£ 15.95

Not Responsible
if seagulls eat
your cake.

No Signs
Allowed!

Welcome
To
Accident

Silly Tongue Twisters

Try and do them all, then see if Mum and
Dad can do better.

I saw Susie sitting in a shoe shine shop.

Can you Can a can as a canner can can a can?

I scream, you scream, we all scream for Ice cream!

If two witches would watch two watches,
which witch would watch which watch?

Fuzzy Wuzzy was a bear. Fuzzy Wuzzy had
no hair. Fuzzy Wuzzy wasn't very Fuzzy, was he?

Round the rough and rugged rocked
the ragged rascal rudely ran.

I have got a date at quarter to eight;
I'll see you at the gate, so don't be late.

Peter Piper picked a peck of pickled peppers.
Did Peter Piper pick a peck of pickled peppers?
If Peter Piper picked a peck of pickled peppers,
where's the peck of
pickled peppers Peter Piper picked?

Tricky Tricks

They're harder than you think.
Ask Mum and Dad to watch.

Walk from one side of the room to the other, with a book on your head. If you can do this gracefully you may be related to Royalty!

Stand on one leg blindfolded for one minute. If you can do this you'll stop wearing both shoes out.

Stand perfectly still for five minutes, you're not allowed to laugh. This is very difficult, and you're very talented if you succeed.

Juggle with three balls. If you can do this you have superb timing.

Eat three crackers in a minute. If you're a crummy athlete, you'll find this impossible.

Get from one side of the room, to the other on your back with an apple on your belly, all the way.

Count to twenty backwards without pausing? If you can do this you're very clever.

Now it's Mum and Dads turn, make sure they don't cheat.

Silly Weather

How do you know if it's been raining cats and dogs?
When you step in a poodle.

Why did the lumberjack wear a helmet?
It was raining Cat's and Logs.

What did one snowman say to the other?
Do you smell carrots?

Why isn't the sky happy on clear days?
Because it has the blues.

How do hurricanes see?
With one eye.

What is wind?
Air in a hurry.

Why is lightning so naughty?
It doesn't know how to conduct itself.

What's a volcano?
A mountain with hiccups.

What type of cloud is so lazy it won't get up?
Fog.

What do clouds wear under their clothes?
Thunderwear.

Man: What's the weather like outside?
Silly Billy: I don't know it's to foggy to see.

My Secrets

Only share with best friends
and Mum and Dad.

Don't tell a soul!

What I'd like to be
when I grow up.
a thecher

My favourite music.
shaceitoff

The Boy/Girl
I want to marry.
Jack

What country
I want to live in.
Phlorda

What I like
to do in my spare
time.
cloler

My favourite colour.
blue

Don't tell a soul!

My Secrets

Only share with best friends
and Mum and Dad.

My prayers.

My answered
prayers.

My favourite
tv program.

My favourite
films.

My favourite
animal.

My favourite
comedian.

Don't tell a soul!

Don't tell a soul!

Don't tell a soul!

Don't tell a soul!

Don't tell a soul!

Don't tell a soul!

Daft Jokes!

What was the
crab sent to jail?
He kept on
pinching things.

How did the police
catch the strawberry
thief?
They caught him
red handed.

What's the safest
way to hammer
nails in?
Get your sister
to hold the nails.

What's are the two
strongest days of the week?
Saturday and
Sunday, because
the others are week days.

What goes
ha-ha-ha-bonk?
A woman laughing
her head off.

What's the difference
between a baker and
an elephant?
One bakes the bread,
the other breaks the bed.

What does a baker
have in common with
a poor man?
They both knead
some dough.

How do you
wake a cockerel?
Set he's alarm cluck.

Sillly Poems

I once knew a Prince
too small
Who loved a Princess
Too tall
He grew sadder and
sadder
Until he found
a ladder
And took it along to
the ball.

Mr Krispell copyright

My Silly Poem

Write it below.

Dads Poem

Write Dad a lovely poem below.

Mums Poem

Write Mum a lovely poem below.

Silly Dinosaurs

What do you call
a dinosaur with
a limp?
My-foot-is-saurus.

What does a T-rex
eat?
Anything he wants.

What do you
call a dinosaur
who won't stop
talking about himself?
A dinobore.

What happened
to the smelly dinosaurs
They became Ex-stinked.

Do dinosaurs
pass exams?
Yes, with extinction.

Why did dinosaurs
eat raw meat?
Because they didn't
know how to cook.

What do you call
a blind dinosaur?
Do-you-think-he-saw-us.

What followed the
dinosaurs?
Their tails.

How do you
ask a dinosaur
to lunch?
Tea Rex?

What do you
call a very articulate
dinosaur?
A theraurus.

Where can you find a dinosaur in a bikini?
At the Dino-shore.

Colour this picture in for Dad!

For a
lovely Dad

Silly Elephants

Why do elephants
paint their toenails
red?
To hide in cherry
trees!

What's the loudest
noise in the
jungle?
Giraffes eating
from cherry trees!

How do you
know if there's an
elephant in your
bed?
You can see the
E on his pyjamas.

Why is an elephant
big grey and wrinkly?
Because if he was
small white and round
he'd be an aspirin.

What should you
give an elephant with
an upset stomach?
Plenty of room.

How do you
fit four elephants
in a mini?
Two in the
front and two
in the back?

How do you
get four monkeys
in a mini?
Ask the elephants
to got out first.

What do you
get if you cross
a mouse with
an elephant?
Big holes in
your skirting board.

If you had two
elephants in a mini
what game would
they be playing?
Squash!

What goes up slowly
and down quickly?
An elephant in
an elevator.

Funny Food

How do you reach
the top of an
ice cream mountain?
With a Jellycopter.

Why shouldn't you
tell an egg a joke?
It might crack up.

What do you call
two banana skins
on the floor?
A pair of slippers.

How can you
make a chicken stew?
Leave it waiting
for hours.

What happens when
you stand on
a grape?
It lets out
a little wine.

Which vegetable goes
best with a
jacket potato?
Button mushrooms.

What biscuit can
fly?
A plane one.

What are the two things
you can't have for
breakfast?
Lunch and supper.

Why did the jelly
wobble?
Because it saw
the milkshake.

Why was the
orange crying?
Because someone hurt
it's peelings.

How do you start a jelly race?
Ready, Set, Go!

Funny Food

Why was the
biscuit sad?
He felt crummy.

Why do all the
vegetables love
the mushroom?
Because he's a
fun-guy.

Why was the
Swiss Cheese praying?
Because he was hole-y.

Why was the small
strawberry crying?
His parents were
in a bit of a jam.

How don you know
of a hamburgers
married.
It wears an onion
ring.

Why was the biscuit
crying?
His mummy had
been a wafer so long.

Why did the plumb
go out with the
raisin.
Because she couldn't
find a date.

What day of the
week do sausages
hate?
Fryday!

What do Rice Krispies
we're on their feet?
Kelloggs.

How do you
make a banana
split?
Cut it in half.

What's yellow and stupid?
Thick custard.

Write the answers above.

Jump in the jellycopter and count the candy in the custard sea, with one eye closed. Time 2 minutes.

Correct answer
Sweet 15
Candy cane 15
Ice cream 12

Daft Jokes

What did the loaf of bread, say to the knife?
You wanna piece of me?

Who one the fight between the bread and the knife?
The knife because the cake was a crummy fighter.

What happened to the rabbits that got married?
They went on a bunny-moon.

How did the two rabbits get back from their bunny-moon.
They caught a plane from the hareport.

What do you get if a bear catches you with a honey jar?
A very sticky situation.

What do get if you cross a crazy hippo with a dessert?
A hippo-potty-mousse

Why do French people eat snails?
Because they don't like fast food.

What do you call a piano with only white keys?
A minor problem.

Dad have you got a good memory?
Yes son, why do you ask?
I've just smashed your shaving mirror.

Ask Mum to help you colour this in.

Our Family Jokes

Write your own favourite family jokes!

Dads

H!dad watdo yousa'l wat

Mums

Grandmas

Grandpas

Brothers

Sisters

Aunts

Uncles

Silly Insects!

What did the fly
say as it hit
the windscreen?
That's me all over.

What's the last
thing that goes
through a wasps
mind when it hits
a windscreen?
It's sting.

Did you hear
about the two
silk worms that
had a race?
It ended in
a tie.

What's the difference
between a bird and
a fly?
A bird can fly but
a fly can't bird.

What's the difference
between school dinners
a slugs?
School dinners come
on a plate.

How do fleas
travel long distance?
By itch hiking.

Why were the flies
playing soccer on a
saucer?
They were practicing
for the cup.

What insect never
leaves you alone?
A stick insect.

Why don't baby
birds smile?
Would you if
your mother fed
you worms all day.

Why did the fly fly?
Because the spider spied her.

Silly Insects!

Where did the spider meet his wife?
On a website.

What do you get if you cross an insect with a baby?
A creepy crawler.

What does a cat sleep on?
A catterpillow.

What's worse than finding a worm in your apple?
Finding half a worm.

First cat: Where have all those fleas gone?
Second cat: Search me.

What do moths study at school?
Mothomatics.

What was the snail doing on the motorway?
A couple of miles a week.

Where do bees go when injured?
Waspital.

How do you tell if a worm is a boy or a girl?
Tell it a joke- if he laughs it's a boy, and if she laughs it's a girl.

What has four wheels and flies?
A garbage truck.

Did you hear about the man ran a successful flea circus?
He started from scratch.

Hidden ladybirds

Find the Eight hidden ladybirds, then colour the picture in for Mum & Dad.

My Favourite Things!

(And I'm not joking)

Write the reasons why!

Mum becuase she cleans my room

Dad becuase he cares me

Best friend Lucy

2nd Best friend Natlia

3rd Best friend Jack

Best Teacher Mrs Gay

2nd Best Teacher Mrs S

If I Ruled The World!

(And I'm not still joking)

Write what you'd do.

Day 1 I'd

Day 2 I'd

Day 3 I'd

Day 4 I'd

Day 5 I'd

Now take a rest you've just changed the world.

Now it's time for Dad to change the world.

Day 1 I'd

Day 2 I'd

Day 3 I'd

Day 4 I'd

Day 5 I'd

Now Dad's running the world, it's a great time
to ask for an increase in pocket money!

Silly riddles!

What's bigger when it's upside down?

The number 6

What has a mouth, and a fork, but never eats?

A river.

What has a tail and a head but no body?

A coin.

How many side has a circle got?

Two- the inside and the outside.

What's in the middle of Paris?

The letter R.

What's black when it's clean and
white when it's dirty?

A blackboard.

What starts with t, ends with t and is
full of tea?

A teapot.

What asks no questions but demands
an answer?

A doorbell.

Jokes to tell your Best Friend

How do eggs leave in an emergency?
Through the fire eggsit.

What type of nuts always have a cold?
Cashews!

What do birds watch on tv?
Duckumentaries!

What birds can you find in Portugal?
Potu-geese!

What's the most slippery country in the world?
Greece!

Teacher: What is a smoke detector used for?
To tell Mum dinners ready.

What do sea monsters eat?
Fish and chips.

How do we know that the Earth won't come to and end?
Because it's round.

How do crabs call their friends?
On shell phones.

Where do you find giant snails?
On the end of a giants fingers.

What's higher than a giraffe?
A giraffes hat.

Jokes to tell your Best Friend

Did you hear about the Dutch women with inflatable shoes?
She popped her clogs.

I can make you talk like a Red Indian.
How?
See I told you.

Doctor, doctor I feel like a bridge.
What's come over you?
Well, so far two lorries, three cars and a bus.

What's snakes favourite subject?
Hiss-story.

Why was Beethoven's fifth favourite fruit?
Ba-na-na-na!

Shall I tell you the joke about the empty house?
There's nothing in it.

Why couldn't the skeleton go to the dance?
He had nobody to go with.

Why is six afraid of seven?
Because seven eight nine!

What's the best way to get straight A's?
Use a ruler.

For my
best friend

Silly School!

Teacher: If I have four apples in one hand and six in the other hand what do I have?
Pupil: Very big hands miss.

Teacher: I hope I didn't see you copy in that test?
Pupil: I hope you didn't, either.

Pupil: I don't think I deserved zero for the school test, sir.
Teacher: Neither do i, but it's the lowest I can give you.

Why was the chicken sent home from school?
For using fowl language.

Teacher: What do you know about Camelot?
Pupil: It's a parking area in the dessert.

Teacher: How did you get that black eye?
Pupil: You see that tree in the playground?
Teacher: Yes.
Pupil: I didn't.

Teacher: What does it mean when the smoke alarm goes off?
Pupil: At this school it means dinners ready.

Teacher: How do you spell education?
Pupil: E-D-U-A-Y-S-H-U-N.
Teacher: That's not how the dictionary spells it.
Pupil: You didn't ask me how the dictionary spells it.

Silly School!

Teacher: If I have four apples in one hand and six in the other hand what do I have?
Pupil: Very big hands miss.

Teacher: I hope I didn't see you copy in that test?
Pupil: I hope you didn't, either.

Pupil: I don't think I deserved zero for the school test, sir.
Teacher: Neither do i, but it's the lowest I can give you.

Why was the chicken sent home from school?
For using fowl language.

Teacher: What do you know about Camelot?
Pupil: It's a parking area in the dessert.

Teacher: How did you get that black eye?
Pupil: You see that tree in the playground?
Teacher: Yes.
Pupil: I didn't.

Teacher: What does it mean when the smoke alarm goes off?
Pupil: At this school it means dinners ready.

Teacher: How do you spell education?
Pupil: E-D-U-A-Y-S-H-U-N.
Teacher: That's not how the dictionary spells it.
Pupil: You didn't ask me how the dictionary spells it.

Silly School!

A boy walked into the school library and said, 'Fish and chips, please.' 'I'm sorry, but this is a library.' 'Sorry,' whispered the pupil, 'Fish and chips please.'

Pupil: Our dog bit four people yesterday so we had to have him put down.
Teacher: Was he mad?
Pupil: Well, he wasn't very happy.

Teacher: Can you tell me what language is spoken in Corsica?
Pupil: Course I can.

Teacher: Mrs Brown, I asked you to come in to discuss Sammy's appearance.
Mrs Brown: Why what's wrong with his appearance?
Teacher: He hasn't made one in my classroom since September.

Teacher: What two days begin with T?
Pupil: Today and tomorrow.

Teacher: Sammy, when's your birthday?
Sammy: May 12th.
Teacher: Which year?
Sammy: Every year.

Pupil: My bird died of flu yesterday?
Teacher: You poor thing, was it bird flu?
Pupil: No, he flew into a car.

Why do magicians do so well in school? They're good at trick questions.

Silly Jokes for Dad

(Don't tell them when Dad's watching sport)

Who's the most wanted criminal in the ocean?
Al Caprawn.
(A Shellfish Criminal)

Who's the second most wanted criminal in the ocean?
Billy the Squid.
(He robbed the riverbank)

Dad: I'm thinking of getting a pig and keeping it in your room?
Teenager: But what about the smell?
Dad: The pig will just have to get used to it.

How do you burn a Silly Billy on the ear?
Phone him up when he's ironing.

Diner: Can I have an elephant sandwich please?
Waiter: I'm sorry, sir, we've run out of bread.

What goes snap, crackle?
Two Rice Krispies.

Passenger: Why has this train stopped?
Guard: We hit a cow, madam.
Passenger: Was it on the track?
Guard: No we had to chase it across a field.

Police arrested two men yesterday, one for drinking battery acid, and one for eating fireworks.
They charged one and let off the other.

Silly Jokes for Dad

(Don't tell them when Dad's watching sport)

What do you get
if you drop a
piano down a coal
mine?
A flat minor.

First man: How many
people work in
your office?
Second man: About
half of them.

What's
black and shoots
out of the ground
shouting knickers?
Crude oil.

What
black and shoots
out of the ground
shouting pants?
Refined oil.

Son: Why haven't you
spoke to Mum all
week?
Dad: Well, son, I don't
like to interrupt her.

Why do bakers
work so hard?
Because they need
the dough.

Patient: Doctor, my hair
is falling out, is there
something you can give
me for it?
Doctor: Ask at reception,
they'll give you a box.

Last night a gigantic
whole suddenly appeared
in the middle of the road.
Don't worry council
workers are looking
into it.

Silly Jokes for Mum

(Don't tell these when Dad's around)

Mum: Dad tried to take me out last night, in a car with wooden doors, wooden wheels, and even a wooden engine.
Son: How was the drive?
Mum: I don't know, it wooden go.

What happened to the snail who lost his shell?
He became very sluggish.

What do you get hanging from banana trees?
Sore arms.

Mum: Dad had a terrible dream last night that he was eating a giant marshmallow?
Son: Whats so terrible about that?
Mum: When he awoke his pillow was missing.

Son: What happens when a car is too clapped out and old to work?
Mum: Someone sells it to Dad.

Where do frogs get there eyes tested?
At the hopician.

What happened when the Granny Smith married the Cox's pipin?
They lived appley ever after.

Son: Dad, will you do my English homework for me tonight?
Dad: No, son, it wouldn't be right.
Son: Well, just do your best.

Son: Mum, Dad says I got my intelligence from him.
Mum: He must be right I've still got mine.

What do you call?

What do you call a girl with a frog on her head?
Lilly.

What do you call a man sitting on your doormat?
Bill.

What do you call a woman with a weight on one side
of her head?
Eileen.

What do you call a man with a spade on his head?
Doug.

What do you call a man without a spade on his head?
Douglas.

What do you call a nun with a washing machine on her head?
Sister-matic.

What do you call a man with a loo on his head?
John.

What do you call a woman with two toilets on her head?
Lulu.

What do you call a woman who stands astride a river?
Bridget.

What do you call a man with no legs?
Neil.

What do you call?

What do you call a cow with two leg?
Lean beef.

What do you call a man floating in the sea?
Bob.

What do you call a deer with no eyes?
No idea.

What do you call a dear with no eyes and no legs?
Still no idea.

What do you call a women who slides
around on a piece of bread?
Marge.

What do you call a man with a jack on his Head?
Jack.

What do you call a man who dunks his
head into his tea?
Duncan.

Why do you call a woman with a tortoise on her head?
Shelly.

What do you call a man with a bag of compost on his head?
Pete.

Silly Monsters!

Did you hear about the monster who cleaned the attic with his girlfriend? Now he can't get the cobwebs out of her fur.

How do you keep a big ugly monster in suspense? I'm not telling you!

Why wouldn't the small zombie go to school? He felt rotten.

What monster always rings the doorbell? The Knock-less-monster.

Why did King Kong eat Big Ben? Because it was time for lunch.

Why did Cyclops give up teaching? He only had one pupil.

What monster lives in a tree? Frank-in-pine.

Where do monsters go to party? To a Scooby-Dooby-Doo.

Why did the Fungi Monster have so many friends? Well, he kind of grew on you in the end.

I dined with a monster I knew
So proud of his big pot of goo
Carrots and bats
Ferrets and rats
I spent the next week on the loo

See if you can copy this sketch.

Silly Birthday's

What did the little candle say to the big candle? You're too young to go out.

What do you get every birthday? A year older.

What do you call an adult balloon? A blown-up.

How can you tell that birthdays are good for you? Because people who live the longest tend to have the most birthdays

Son: Dad what's the easiest way to remember mums birthday? Dad: Forget it once.

What if no one comes to your birthday party? You can have your cake and eat it.

What did the clam do on his birthday? He shellybrated.

Where can you find a great birthday present for a cat? In a Cat-alogue.

What has long wings, a long tail and wears a bow? A birthday Pheasant.

Were any famous men born on your birthday? No only babies.

What do you call a crazy balloon? A balloonatic.

Balloonatic

What crazy balloon escaped from
The balloonatic asylum?

Balloonatic
Asylum

Silly Snow!

What do snowmen wear
on their heads?
Ice caps.

What do snowmen
call their offspring?
Chill-dren.

Where do snowmen go
to dance?
To Snowballs.

Wear Did Jack Frost
meet his wife?
On the winter-net.

How does a snowman
get to work?
By icicle.

Where do snowmen
keep their money?
In the snowbank.

What kind of money
do snowmen use?
Ice lolly.

What did the executioner
say to his mother?
Only twenty chopping
days to Christmas.

Why is an armchair
like a Christmas dinner?
Because it's full off
stuffing.

What side of a Robin
has the most
feathers?
The outside.

Silly Riddles

What's hidden in the pictures?

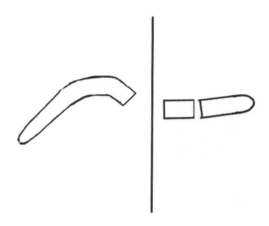

A worm crossing over a razor blade.

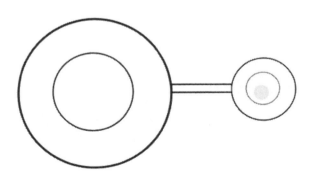

A Mexican frying a egg.

Silly Riddles

What's hidden in the pictures?

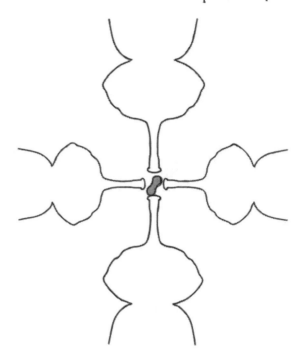

Four Elephants trying to e a peanut.

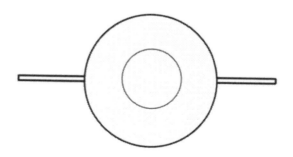

A Mexican riding a bike.

Silly Princess

Cinderella: Oh Dear the ugly sisters fell down the wishing well last night?
Prince: I didn't know wishing wells worked!

Why did Snow White treat all dwarfs equally?
Because she was the fairest of all of them.

What did the prince sing to the mermaid?
'Salmond-enchanted-evening!

Why did Pinocchio leave Cinderella?
Because he said she was just stringing him along.

Why was Snow White thrown out of the soccer team?
She kept on running away from the ball.

Prince: Ugly sister why is your nose so swollen?
Ugly sister: I was smelling a brose.
Prince: There no B in brose.
Ugly sister: There was in this one.

What did Cinderella's fish wear to the ball?
Glass flippers.

What did the seven dwarfs sing whilst working in the butchers?
Gristle while you work.

Daft Jokes!

Where on a ship
do you find sailors
laughing?
Where the funnel be!

When were there
only three vowels in
the alphabet?
A long time ago,
before U and I
born.

What cows live
in the North Pole?
Friesian cows.

Where can you grow
space carrots?
In force fields.

What do you
call a nude man
on a high wire?
A tension-seeker.

Where does an
iron live?
With his flat mates.

Why do you
call a duck that
goes Bang! Then lights
up the sky?
A firequaker.

Why was the
frog sent to
jail?
He Kermited a crime.

What's the first words a
baby computer says?
Data!

Thank you for
purchasing this book.
If you enjoyed it
please give it
a review!

Printed in the United States of America

First Printing, 2018

Contact. Sniffitysnoo302@gmail.com

I can highly recommend...

Mr Krispell's Kids Joke Book!

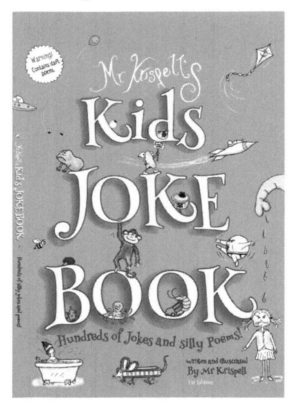

What's got big ears, a tail and
squeaks when you blow into it?
A Mouse-organ!
Mr Krispell's Kids Joke Book
contains hundreds of new jokes,
classic jokes and hilariously
daft poems, wonderfully illustrated.

Made in the USA
Middletown, DE
19 December 2018